COVER |

Samory Toure is a legendary African Muslim king in Guinea who is celebrated for the empire he founded and his fierce resistance fighting against French colonialism. A towering monument of Toure was built near a small roundabout near downtown Conakry. This important historic site is a reminder to Guineans of their ancestors' struggles for independence from France. Toure was also the great-grandfather of Guinea's first President Sekou Toure.

Photo Attribution: https://commons.wikimedia.org/w/index.php?curid=615378

COUNTRY JUMPER in Guinea

Copyright © 2021

All rights reserved. No part of this book may be used or reproduced in any manner whatsoever without written permission, except in the case of reprints in the context of review.

Contact Author at:
countryjumperbooks@gmail.com

Website:
countryjumperbooks.net

Hello boys and girls! Do you know how many countries are in the world today? The answer will depend a lot on how a "country" is defined. Some countries are members of the United Nations, others are not, and some are given only partial recognition. However, they are just as important to learn about. Which country do you live in?

My name is COUNTRY JUMPER, and I'd like you to come and jump with me around the world. I've selected 205 countries to visit, so put on your Jumping Shoes and buckle up. Today we are visiting Guinea, a country in the continent of Africa.

Table of Contents

Chapter 1: Facts

Chapter 2: Terrain and Climate

Chapter 3: Politics

Chapter 4: Education

Chapter 5: Transportation

Chapter 6: Holidays and Festivals

Chapter 7: Animal, Bird, and Flower

Chapter 8: Popular Foods

Chapter 9: Money

Chapter 10: Sports

Chapter 11: Music and Instruments

Chapter 12: Clothing

Chapter 13: Fun Places for Kids to Visit

Chapter 14: Other Interesting Facts

Facts About Guinea

Around 900 BCE, the Soussou (also Susu or Soso) came to the area, and their kingdom succeeded during the 12th to 13th centuries, until the Islamic Mali Empire took over the region. When the Mali Empire began to decline in the 15th century, it was replaced by its vassal states. The most successful of these states was the Songhai Empire which eventually surpassed the Mali Empire in both territory and wealth. The Songhai Empire prospered until a civil war weakened it, and it fell to invaders from Morocco. The Moroccans were unable to rule the kingdom effectively, and it split into many small kingdoms. The slave trade came to the coastal region of Guinea with the Europeans in the 16th century. The Fulani Empire dominated the area between the 16th and 19th centuries. France entered the region intending to colonize West Africa and convert countries into a French state and claimed Guinea as a protectorate in 1849. The protectorate was first called Rivires du Sud, and was later renamed French Guinea. Slavery was abolished in the country around 1865. Before 1882, the coastal areas of Guinea were part of the French colony of Senegal. In 1891 France declared Guinea to be a colony, separate from Senegal. France defeated Guinea in 1898, and Guinea became part of the French West African Federation. The French Fourth Republic collapsed in 1958 due to political instability and its failures in dealing with its colonies. France's colonies were given a choice between more autonomy in a new French community or immediate independence. Guinea declared its independence from France on October 2, 1958. The capital of Guinea is Conakry. The estimated population in early 2021 was approximately 13,419,600.

The flag of Guinea was adopted in 1958. This vertical tricolor flag is red, green, and yellow. The flag is based on the pan-African colors and is very similar to the flag of Ghana, with the colors in the same order. Ghana's flag has a star in the center of the yellow stripe, and the stripes are horizontal instead of vertical. The red color in the flag represents the bloodshed of the people who struggled for freedom and independence. Yellow symbolizes the mineral wealth of the country and the sun. The green stripe represents the lush vegetation in the country.

Guinea's present coat of arms was adopted in 1993. It features a dove carrying a golden olive branch in its beak. The three colors of the national flag, red, yellow, and green, are located inside the shield. A ribbon displaying the national motto: Travail, Justice, Solidarite (Work, Justice, Solidarity), appears below the shield. The arms formerly also included a crossed sword and rifle. A 1958 version featured a red and green shield with a yellow elephant on it.

A country's national coat of arms is a symbol that signifies an independent state in the form of a heraldic achievement. An important use for national coats of arms is as the main symbol on the cover of passports.

Guinea's constitution prohibits religious discrimination and provides for the right of individuals to choose their religious faith. The official language of Guinea is French, which was inherited from colonial rule. French serves as a medium of instruction in the schools, and it is also the language used by the government, administration, and media. Indigenous languages include Fula, Malinké, Susu, Kissi, Kpelle, and Toma. Fulu is spoken by around 40 percent of the population, who reside mainly in Middle Guinea.

Islam is the majority religion in Guinea, with approximately 85 percent of the population being Muslim. Most Muslims are Sunnis who follow the Maliki tradition and Tijani Sufi order. Islam was introduced into Guinea through the Mali Empire. Around eight percent of the population are Christians, which include Evangelicals, Protestants, Roman Catholics, and Seventh-Day Adventists. Muslims and Christians incorporate indigenous African beliefs into their religious practices. Jehovah's Witnesses are also active in Guinea and recognized by the government.

Grand Mosque in Conakry

Terrain and Climate of Guinea

Guinea is bordered by Guinea-Bissau, Senegal, Mali, Cte d'Ivoire, Liberia, and Sierra Leone. Its terrain is generally flat coastal plain, mountainous region, a savanna interior, and forested area in the Guinea Highlands. Several of the region's major rivers originate from Guinea's highlands, making it the water tower of West Africa. The coastal region and most of the inland have a tropical climate. Guinea experiences a monsoonal-type rainy season from April to November, with high temperatures, southwesterly winds, and high humidity.

Photo 187759204 © Igor Gromov | Dreamstime.com

Politics of Guinea

Guinea's government is in the early stages of a transition from decades of authoritarian rule. It has a constitutional democratic republic framework. The government exercises executive power, and legislative power is entrusted to both the government and the National Assembly. The president is normally elected by popular vote for a seven-year term. The president is assisted by a council of 25 civilian ministers who he appoints. Guinea's legal system is based on French civil laws, with local additions that can be modified.

National Assembly in Conakry
Image from https://commons.wikimedia.org/w/index.php?curid=432366

Education in Guinea

Guinea's constitution of 1958 guarantees free and compulsory education to children until age 15. Children go through six years of primary and seven years of secondary school. Secondary education is also offered as a six-year program. Instruction is offered in French and local languages. Girls, especially, are deprived of an education since they are required to help out at home or may get married at an early age. The Kofi Annan University is a private university in Conakry, and it is one of the most prestigious and oldest institutions of higher education in Guinea.

Kofi Annan University

Transportation in Guinea

Transportation in Guinea consists of road, taxi, and air. There is no bus service nor passenger rail, and the rest of the transportation is relatively unreliable. Over 50 percent of the national road network is described as inadequate. Guinean vehicles are also poorly maintained, with many of them lacking functional lights, making night travel dangerous. Shared taxis which charge per seat are common for locals in Guinea. They are used for transport from city to city. Another way to travel is by taxi bikes, which are faster and more comfortable. Conakry International Airport is the largest airport in the country.

Holidays and Festivals in Guinea

The Feast of Sacrifice, also known as Eid Al Adha, is the most important feast on the Muslim calendar. Within the Muslim world, this holiday is celebrated as a tribute to the Prophet Abraham's who was willing to sacrifice everything for God. The exact day is based on lunar sightings, and therefore the date may vary. During the Feast of Sacrifice, Muslims sacrifice a cow or ram to reenact Abraham's obedience to God. The family eats a third of the meal they've prepared, and a third goes to friends and relatives. The leftover food, around a third, is donated to the poor and needy.

The Macao Festival in Guinea is one of the most highly anticipated events of the year. It is celebrated with much display and enthusiasm. The festival is held in March-April and is based on an old legend about a hunter's search for a drumming monkey. The event is celebrated with a circus, where a mix of acts based on native traditions are performed by a group of acrobats, dancers, jugglers, and musicians. The display of local talent is entertaining for the entire family.

Animal, Bird, Flowers of Guinea

The elephant is the national animal of Guinea. There are two species of elephants found in Africa; the African forest elephant and the African bush elephant. The African bush elephant is slightly bigger than the African forest elephant. Guinea's national animal is the African forest elephant. This animal has grey skin and is sparsely covered with coarse black hair. The elephant's trunk is used for smelling, touching, feeding, drinking, producing sounds, defending, and attacking.

Image by Peter H. Wrege @ https://commons.wikimedia.org/w/index.php?curid=12291072

Guinea has not designated a national bird; however, it is home to an impressive number of bird species. Some of these birds stay all-year-round, while others spend a good part of the growing season in Guinea to breed and raise their young. The white-breasted guineafowl is a bird species that is found in Guinea. This bird is medium-sized and is a terrestrial bird of the guineafowl family. The white-breasted guineafowl has black plumage with a bare red head, white breast, black tail, greenish-brown bill, and greyish feet. It feeds mainly on seeds, berries, termites, and small animals.

Photo 197270602 © Dawn Quadling | Dreamstime.com

Guinea's national flower was voted on in 2018. The plant of the Vernonia djalonensis is fuschia-colored, and it has the appearance of a spineless thistle. It is found in the Fouta Djallo mountains of central Guinea in one location. This unusual bloom is a robust perennial soft-stemmed undershrub, with crowded leaves and broad flowerheads. It spreads 3/4 inches across when it opens. The Vernonia djalonensis can be used as a medicinal plant and is used against colds. This plant is critically endangered and is threatened with planned housing development.

Popular Foods of Guinea

The national dish of Guinea is poulet yassa, which originated from Senegal. This is a simple chicken dish that is popular in West Africa. The chicken pieces are fried until they are golden brown and cooked throughout. The chicken can also be baked. Onions and spices are sautéd to make a caramelized sauce, which is poured over the chicken and simmered together. The onion and lemon-infused marinade tenderize the meat of the chicken. Poulet yassa is typically served with rice.

Typical Guinean cuisine often includes the traditional dish of fou-fou. Fou-fou is very common in many African countries. The term fou-fou refers to ground provision (tubular root vegetables) that has been boiled, pounded or mashed and formed into balls. The traditional method of preparing fou-fou is by mixing equal portions of mashed cassava and green plantain flour with water. The mixture can be adjusted by either increasing or decreasing the thickness of the fou-fou. This dish is often served with various types of soups.

Image by Flixtey @ https://commons.wikimedia.org/w/index.php?curid=28530134

Patates is a traditional African dish that originated from Guinea. The ingredients include a combination of sweet potatoes, oil, and salt. The sweet potatoes are sliced into wedges, seasoned with salt, and fried in hot oil until crisp. The result is a deep orange-colored sweet snack. Patates are often served with an oily sauce made from tomatoes, onions, and fish sauce. There is also a southern Guinean variation of patates called loco, where the plantain chunks are fried in palm oil. Patates are sold as a snack in markets and on roadsides.

Money in Guinea

The Guinean franc (Code: GNF) is the currency of Guinea. It replaced the CFA franc, which was used until 1959. In 1971, the Guinean franc was replaced by syli; however, it was reintroduced as the country's currency in 1985, at par with the syli. Although the Guinean franc is subdivided into one hundred centimes, no centime denominations were ever issued. Frequently used banknotes are in denominations of 100, 500, 1,000, 2,000, 5,000, 10,000, and 20,000 francs. Rarely used banknotes are 25 and 50 francs. Coins are in denominations of 1, 5, 10, 25, and 50 francs. Coins were minted in aluminum bronze.

Image by Joelguinea @ https://commons.wikimedia.org/w/index.php?curid=4019633

Sports in Guinea

Football (soccer) is the most popular sport in Guinea. The Fédération Guinéenne de Football runs the association, administers the national football team and the national league. The country's national football team has played international football since 1962. The football team has won the Amilcar Cabral Cup five times. Leather soccer balls are hard to find in Guinea, and children get creative and make their own balls out of plastic bags, rags, or newspapers. Some other recreational activities include athletics, basketball, biking, karate, and rugby.

Music and Instruments of Guinea

Guinea is one of the best places for music in West Africa. Guinean music is mainly known for the dance bands of the 1970s. Those and other styles are firmly rooted in the traditions of West Africa's hereditary praise singers (Mande jelis). Guineans play a wide variety of string and percussion instruments. These include the balafon, kora (a hybrid of a lute and harp), guitar, and n'goni. The dunun and djembe drums are also used in folk music.

Balafon
Image by Redmedea @ https://commons.wikimedia.org/w/index.php?curid=1755997

Traditional Clothing in Guinea

Traditional clothing in Guinea is similar to other countries in West Africa. Although clothing styles may differ depending on ethnicity, most outfits tend to be loose and conservative. Traditionally, men wear a long, flowing, wide-sleeved robe called a boubou. It is worn with pants that are tapered at the mid-calf. Women wear long dresses or loose tops with long skirts. They also wear a pull-over robe called a kaftan which is similar to the boubou.

Kaftan

Fun Places for Kids to Visit in Guinea

At the Centre d'Art Acrobatique Keita Fodeba, visitors can watch performers rehearse. The center produces some of Africa's most talented acrobats and contortionists. This is one of the most amazing experiences that Guinea has to offer. Every weekday acrobats flip, spin, and twirl through routines that have made them the envy of circuses all over the world. The center's success has made these young performers sought out worldwide to participate in circus performances.

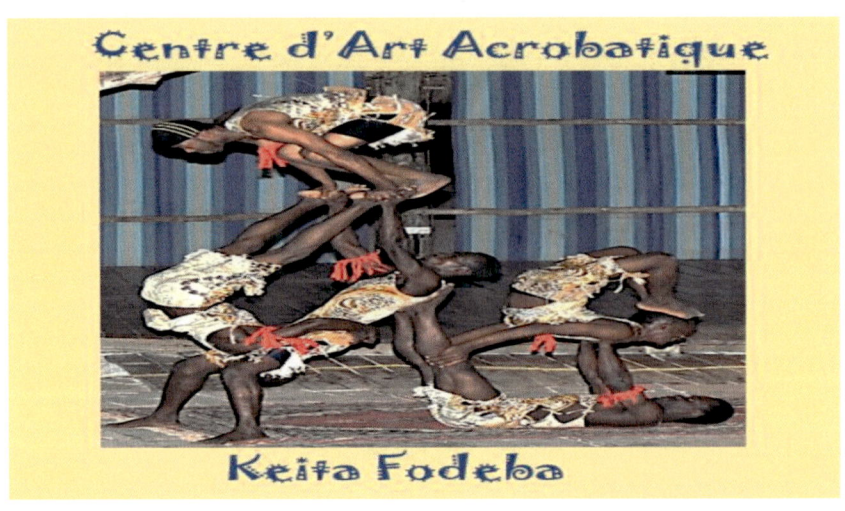

The National Museum in Guinea has a remarkable collection of artifacts, statues, masks, ancient musical instruments, and models. These exhibits reflect the daily life of Guinean farmers and fishers. There is also a gallery where items such as fabrics, traditional costumes, wooden statues, and embossed Tuareg leather are for sale. Although the museum is not very big, its contents are rich in the Guineans' cultural heritage. Visitors will get to listen to stories that will allow them to appreciate this West African country's cultural journey.

Guinea has several waterfalls that come in various sizes and types, and waterfalls are among the country's greatest attractions. Some give off a small trickle, while others have thundering cascades. The Chutes de Ditinn is the highest and most impressive waterfall that pushes waves of water crashing off a 120-meter sandstone cliff. Many monkeys and birds of prey frequent this spectacular plunge of water. Visitors are rewarded with a swim in the pool after a short hike down to the bottom.

Photo 186110741 © TravelTelly | Dreamstime.com

Other Interesting Facts About Guinea

- Guinea was known as French Guinea before it became the Republic of Guinea.
- Guinea is on the Atlantic Ocean.
- Much of Guinea is made up of jungle.
- Despite its natural wealth, Guinea is one of the ten poorest countries in the world.
- Guinea is one of the least developed countries in the world.
- The country is sometimes referred to as Guinea-Conakry to distinguish it from other countries, such as Guinea-Bissau and Equatorial Guinea.
- Guinea has 25% of the world's known bauxite reserves.
- Guinea has absorbed over 150,000 refugees from Sierra Leone following cross-border conflicts.
- Conakry contains almost 25% of the total population of Guinea.
- Diamonds and gold are significant natural resources in Guinea.
- Electricity is not available to many Guineans, and service is intermittent for those fortunate to have it, even in the capital city of Conakry.
- Africa's fourth-largest mosque is in Guinea.
- Eighty percent of Guinea's population works in agriculture.

Guinea-Bissau is the next country on our journey. I hope you like cashews. ***Guinea-Bissau*** is the sixth-largest producer of cashews in the world. The air travel distance between Guinea and ***Guinea-Bissau*** is approximately 394 miles. It will take around 0.7 hours to arrive.

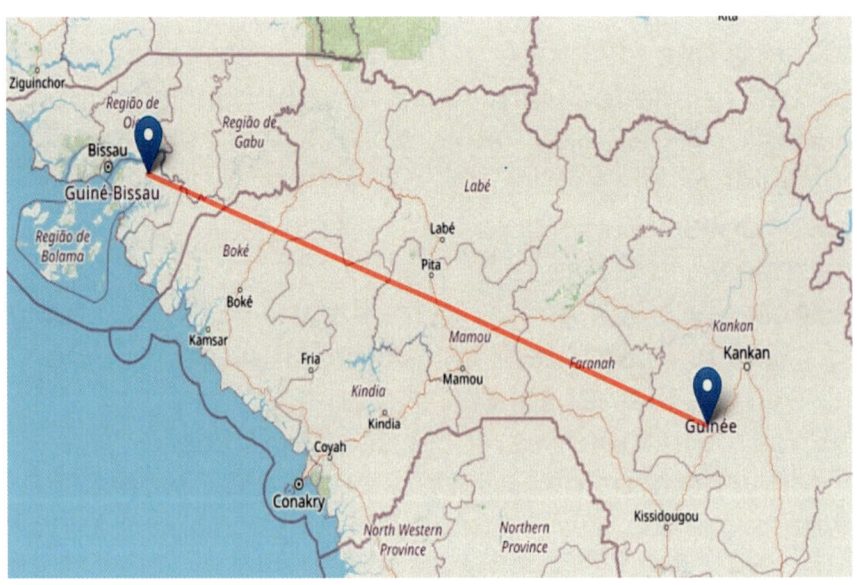

REFERENCES

1. https://www.adequatetravel.com/blog/most-visited-monuments-in-guinea/
2. https://www.afrika-junior.de/content/continent/guinea.htm
3. https://en.wikipedia.org/wiki/Guinea
4. http://mapsopensource.com/guinea
5. https://flagpedia.net/guinea
6. https://www.worldatlas.com/flags/guinea
7. https://www.worldatlas.com/articles/what-languages-are-spoken-in-the-republic-of-guinea.html
8. http://languesafricaines.blogspot.com/
9. https://www.worldatlas.com/articles/religious-beliefs-in-guinea-conakry.html
10. https://www.studycountry.com/guide/GN-education.htm
11. https://www.worldnomads.com/travel-safety/western-africa/guinea/guinea-entry-and-internal-travel
12. https://wikitravel.org/en/Guinea
13. https://www.officeholidays.com/holidays/guinea/eid-al-adha
14. https://www.iexplore.com/articles/travel-guides/africa/guinea/festivals-and-events
15. https://einfon.com/nationalsymbols/national-animal-symbol-of-guinea/
16. https://en.wikipedia.org/wiki/White-breasted_guineafowl
17. https://www.kew.org/blogs/kew-science/guinea-the-campaign-for-a-national-flower
18. http://plants.jstor.org/compilation/Vernonia.djalonensis
19. https://nationalfoods.org/recipe/national-dish-of-guinea-poulet-yassa/
20. https://en.wikipedia.org/wiki/Fufu
21. https://www.tasteatlas.com/patates
22. https://en.wikipedia.org/wiki/Guinean_franc
23. https://www.topendsports.com/world/countries/guinea.htm
24. https://www.worldmusic.net/guide/music-of-guinea/
25. https://www.vagabondjourney.com/clothing-in-guinea/
26. https://www.lonelyplanet.com/guinea/conakry/attractions/centre-dart-acrobatique-keita-fodeba/a/poi-sig/1554732/355327
27. https://www.lonelyplanet.com/guinea/top-things-to-do/a/poi/355319
28. http://afrotourism.com/attraction/national-museum-of-guinea/
29. http://justfunfacts.com/interesting-facts-about-guinea/
30. https://www.distancefromto.net/distance-from-guinea-to-guinea-bissau

Continue following *COUNTRY JUMPER* as he treks across the globe from countries A through Z. Why stop here when there is so much more to learn about this great big world? Where will the next jump take you? You can follow *COUNTRY JUMPER* on his journey from A through Z or jump into the countries that you are curious to learn more about. A total of 205 books representing each country will be available in this series. If you cannot find a country that you would like to explore, please contact the author.

Happy reading!

Made in the USA
Middletown, DE
15 December 2022